AF448049

And Their Heartfelt Response..

JANICE STAMPLEY ALLEN

WHAT WOMEN WANT TO KNOW ABOUT MEN
AND THEIR HEARTFELT RESPONSE
Copyright © 2024 Janice Trenice Stampley.

No part of this publication may be reproduced, distributed, or transmitted in any form or by any means, including photocopying, recording, or other electronic or mechanical methods, without the prior written permission of the publisher, except in the case of brief quotations embodied in reviews and certain other non-commercial uses permitted by copyright law.

Because of the dynamic nature of the Internet, any web addresses or links contained in this book may have changed since publication and may no longer be valid. The views expressed in the work are solely those of the author and do not necessarily reflect the views of the publisher, and the publisher hereby disclaims any responsibility for them.

Any people depicted in stock imagery provided by Getty images are models, and such images are being used for illustrative purposes only.

Printed in the United States of America

Dedication

To my Lord and Savoir Jesus Christ
My loving family
And the late Hardy James Sr. & Jr.
and Dorothy Mae Stampley

Preface

Women have been curious since the beginning of time about issues dealing with matters of the heart. After being blessed to write and publish 6 books titled "Poetry for the soul vol. 1, 2 & 3 "A search for love "Resisting Temptation" and Children's bedtime stories I felt it would be interesting tofind out how men really feel when it comes to matters of the heart. This book was carefully put together so that women could get the answers to questions that have caused them so much heartache & pain for many generations. In formulating this1 book, I asked 30 different women to give me a heartfelt question that they would like to be answered by men. to get the answers I needed I had to interview 30 to 40 men from different ethnic groups & backgrounds. As a result I have written a book "titled What women want to know about men," in hope it can give women all around the world the answers to the many heartfelt questions they have always wanted to know about men.

What WOMEN want to know About MEN

And Their Heartfelt Response

Over the years I've come to realize that men and women around the world will always have a difference of opinion when it comes to matters of the heart.

When God created man, he named him Adam, and gave him access to everything in the garden of Eve except for one apple tree, which down the line will play a key role in the lives of both men and women for generations to come. The narrative of this story derives from a period when Adam becames lonely, and God takes one of his ribs and creates a woman for him as a companion whom he named "Eve." Adam was being submissive to Eve because she had been given to him as a companion; but one day after being tempted in the garden, Eve deceived Adam and caused God to throw them both out of the Garden of Eve. This act of deception proved women have been deceiving and manipulative ever since the beginning of time. Since man was the most dominant of the two, he formed his own opinion of how women should be treated. It didn't take long for women to realize they weren't being treated right and eventually became defiant to their men. Subsequently, their difference of opinions will only cause them lots of heartache and pain down the line.

Still today after many generations have passed there are still lots of people dealing with the very same issues of the heart. Therefore, to help simplify matters, I felt it was time to come forth and ask men of different calibers some of the most evasive questions that has caused women so much heartache and pain ever since the beginning of time. Hopefully, by gaining this information it could help women everywhere better understand why men respond and react the way they do when it comes to matters of the heart.

I spent several months talking to diverse types of women trying to find out what were some of their most heartfelt concerns when it pertained to matters of the heart. I was shocked to find out that most of the women, regardless of their generation had the very same concerns. However, while doing my research I realized if men were asked personal questions such as these, they would probably not feel comfortable answering them truthfully. Therefore, I decided to form a questionnaire whereas the men could answer the questions truthfully without worrying about revealing their identity. Once the surveys were finalized, I couldn't believe how many men were willing to participate and answer the questions that women so desperately wanted to know. It was then I realized that men as well as women were curious about how the opposite sex felt when it came to matters of the heart.

■ The first question asked was (1.) Why do men cheat when they have a good woman?

Out of all the men interviewed, most of them replied "It was strictly casual sex, it had nothing to do with their woman." They also said since women are so quick to sleep around, it not only gave them a chance to indulge in different conversations but to feel something different sexually as well. However, some men did say "despite the temptation, if they had a good woman they would never cheat."

These answers didn't set right with women, and they responded by saying regardless of why a man cheats, it's totally unacceptable. Women felt, "loyalty plays a big role in being a good woman and if you're being faithful to your man, he should be faithful to you as well."

■ The next question asked was (2) How can a man abuse (hurt) his woman by cheating and still claim to love her?

Most men didn't want to comment on this question, but for the ones that did reply said, "when a man is cheating, he's only thinking about himself and the pleasure he's getting at that time." Some of the other men replied, "Just because a man cheat doesn't mean he's in love with the woman." For example, a man could truly be in love with his woman and still end up falling weak for another woman and give in to temptation.

Men also looks at some women as being jump offs, which to a man is someone they can sleep with without any commitment. However, women replied "abuse is mental as well as physical and even though a man may never physically hit a woman, he may have still administered some form of mental abuse whether he knows it or not." For example, a man can say something hurtful to a woman and it will stick with her throughout their relationship. And as far as them cheating there's no way a man can really love a woman and share his most intimate being with someone else, because to a woman this is considered the worst kind of betrayal.

■ The next question asked was (3) Why are men so scared of commitment?

Most men said they aren't scared of commitment they just don't want to be tied down to the same woman all the time, and being committed means they would have to give up everything and just be with that one person. And some said "being in a committed relationship only made them miserable, and they would rather be single whereas they can be able to deal with whomever they choose. But women don't like to be known as a friend, that's why they strive to get men to commit. Women believe if they have a title, it gives them the authority to voice their opinion when it comes to their relationship.

■ The next question asked was (4) What makes your man stop wanting to make love to you?

Most men said there are many things that could cause them to stop making love to their woman, such as lack of communication, the spark has gone out of their relationship, or they just no longer find her attractive. Some men even said their woman had gotten lazy and didn't want to try anything different, and as a result, it caused them to become sexually depressed. But regardless of their reasons, it always ended up with the men cheating and getting sexually satisfied by someone else. But women feel like men should talk to them first and find out what's causing the dramatic change in their mood and give them a chance to fix the problem before they go out and cheat, because it could be something as simple as stress from taking care of the kids or extra responsibility between home and work.

■ The next question asked was (5) Why is it so hard for men to spend quality time with their woman?

Most men said they wouldn't have a problem spending quality time with their woman if she didn't want to talk so much. For example, men can hang with other men for hours without saying a word, but when they try to spend time with their woman, she wants to constantly ask questions that will eventually lead to an argument.

But women consider quality time as a time to chill with their man and catch up on where they stand in their relationship, and to see if he still feels the same way he did when they first met.

■ The next question was (6) How would you know if a man is truly in love with you?

Most men said that a woman would know if he's truly in love with her through his verbal and physical display of affection and by the length he would go to make her happy. Men also said they display their love by spending every moment they can around her. Oddly, when it came to this question women somewhat felt the same as the men. They felt if a man truly loved them, he would shower them with compliments and do everything in his power to make them feel as if they were the only woman in the world.

■ The next question asked was (7) Why do men treat women in the streets better than their own?

Most men said they don't feel like they treat women in the street better than their own, because they financially and emotionally provide everything their woman needs whereas, the women in the street basically does the same things as his woman but only gets a few dollars and some sex. But women don't feel like their man should give another woman anything because it's worst enough he's cheating and betraying her but he's taking money from their home also.

■ The next question asked was (8) How can a man start dating someone so quick after leaving a long-term relationship?

Most men said if they started dating someone right after ending a long-term relationship it would be because they were already cheating and no longer had feelings for who they were with. Some men also said they felt the need to be emotionally attached to someone, because it not only kept them from being alone, but it helped ease the pain from their former relationship as well. They also added if a man gets with a woman strictly for emotional support, nine times out of ten he is likely to end up leaving her and returning to his previous relationship. But everyone knows the heart don't change just because the mind does, and if a man truly loved the woman, he would've given their relationship a chance to see if it could be rekindled before moving on to someone new. But there's no reason a man should've started dating right after a relationship ended, because just like it takes time to fall in love, it should've taken the same amount of time to get over them.

So regardless, of what reason a man says he's in another relationship, there's no way he should've been able to get over someone he's shared years of his life with.

■ The next question asked was (9) Why do men treat cheating differently when it comes to their woman?

Most men said they are very territorial when it comes to another man sleeping with their women, and it would become physical because of their pride. And even though women react differently than men it doesn't mean they don't feel the same way; women hurt just as much as men do, and that's why men should realize what's good for the goose is good for the gander. So, if men know cheating can cause all this pain they shouldn't issue it, especially if they don't want to feel it themselves.

■ The next question asked was (10) Why is it so hard for men to show their true feelings?

Most of the men said as they grew from boys to men, they were taught that they should be hard to impress women. For example, boys were always told that they shouldn't cry, nor should they show weakness when it comes to women, because if they show how they really feel women would say they are soft and try to use them. For instance, some men said because of past relationships they've learned not to be so quick to show their true feelings, because once the woman saw he would do anything for her, she ended up using him. But woman already know that under that hard exterior all men are soft, because once their hearts involved no matter how hard they portray to be their true feeling will always show whether it's good or bad.

■ The next question asked was (11) What is a definite sign of an unfaithful man?

Most men said obvious signs of an unfaithful man are a change in his behavior, excessive lying, hiding his phone, and going from being a homebody to hanging out all the time. But they feel the most obvious is when they claim to work late and start coming home with the smell of an unfamiliar perfume or a different shade of lipstick on their clothing. But despite all the signs that men may think; to a woman the most definite sign is that gut feeling she gets in her stomach after he starts leaving home for hours at a time. And whether she choose to acknowledge her feelings or not she will know it's true because a definite side effect will be the constant mood swings.

■ The next question was (12) What attracts a man to a woman?

Men had varied reasons for what attracts them to women such as her personality, conversation, independency, appearance, and lastly what she has going for herself such as a car, house and job. But women said men should stop being so choosy and make something happen for themselves and stop looking for someone to take care of them. We all know that because beauty comes from within, and if men would stop trying to run game all the time and get to know the women better then maybe they could find someone they could build a strong relationship with.

■ The next question asked was (13) What can a woman do to push a man away?

Most men said there are lots of things a woman can do to push them away such as complaining, withholding sex, lying, being sneaky, cheating or just being lazy. But out of all the complaints most of the men agreed they could not stand a nagging woman. Men said women are drama queens by nature and they would rather leave the relationship and be lonely before they would want to hear a woman nagging all the time. However, women already know that men think of them as drama queens, and sadly we must agree that most women are guilty of what they say. But sometimes men can exaggerate, for example we can ask our man a simple question and because they don't want to answer it, they would say we're nagging.

■ The next question asked was (14) How can a man determine if a woman is wife material?

Men said there are many factors they look for in determining if a woman is marriage material such as how she carries herself in public, her appearance, her conversation, independence, whether she's classy or hood and how much baggage she has, but most of all they look at how easy the woman is because her respect level goes a long way especially if she's being considered as someone they're planning on spending the rest of their life with.

To be honest all women aren't marriage material because some women are outgoing and enjoy being single, and some are home bodies which are normally the ones men will end up choosing as their wives, because at the end of the day a man wants a woman that will cook and pamper them like their mothers did.

■ The next question asked was (15) Why do men stay in a relationship and cheat instead of just leaving?

Most men said even though they cheat they don't plan to leave their home because they still care about the person they are with, and some said if they had children with the woman, they've found it's cheaper to stay in the relationship. But most women feel if the man is already cheating the relationship is already over, and if he continues to stay, he will only cause the relationship to become more dysfunctional than it already is, and eventually it will start affecting the children as well.

■ The next question asked was (16) How do men define "Love"?

Men said "love" to them is being emotionally and physically attracted to someone to the point they would do anything for them. They also said if they love someone it makes them want to spend all their free time with them. Shockingly, women feel the same way, but they feel quality time plays a big role also, but most of all they want men to respect them and treat them like the queens they are.

■ The next question asked was (17) Why do men get jealous when other men are interested in their woman?

Some men said they get a little insecure when other men are talking to their woman because they know the things that men say when they're trying get a woman to sleep with them. But women feel if a man was taking care of his woman like he should there's no reason to be insecure, because no matter what a man say's he can't do any more than she allows.

■ The next question was (18) Why are men so intimidated by strong minded women?

Most men said strong minded women are too independent and self-sufficient, and therefore they don't know how to play their role as a woman and let the man be the man. But women believe men just want them to be weak and needy so they can control the relationship, and if a woman is independent, they know she don't need them, and they can't control her like they want too.

■ The next question was (19) Why do men stay with a woman because she looks good?

Some men said they look at a good-looking woman as being a trophy piece, and it feels good to have her on their side even though she has nothing else to offer. But women feel life is too short to compromise with your happiness for any reason, and a man must be very insecure if he'll settle for being miserable just to have a good-looking woman on his side.

■ The next question asked was (20) How can a woman tell if a man is just using her?

Most men said they wouldn't want to spend time with her unless she had money or something that could benefit them, and after they've gotten what they wanted they would find an excuse to leave. But a woman already knows when a man is using her because he never offers to take her anywhere and every time, he comes by he's always asking for something, but never willing to give her anything in return.

■ The next question was (21) How can men take care of another woman's child and not take care of his own?

Most men said when they enter a new relationship, they are required to take care of their new family which may include children. They said how can a woman say they've abandoned their children when every time she gets mad, she uses the children as leverage and won't let him see them. But women feel even though some women act this way men should still try to do everything in their power to make sure their own children are still being properly taken care of also.

■ The next question was (22) Why do men cheat after they get married?

Most men said after they got married their wives got too comfortable and stopped satisfying them sexually, and others said they were forced to get married and wasn't in love with the woman. But the most common one of all was the man married the woman for reasons such as kids, sex, or physical attraction. But men must realize that marriage require more responsibility than just dating, and sometimes it causes the woman to no longer have the time and energy to put into fulfilling her husband sexual appetite like she once did.

■ The next question was (23) Why do men tell unnecessary lies?

Most men said it's to protect themselves from something they're doing or to avoid an argument. And some said they lie to keep the women interested in them. But women just want men to be real with them, but for some reason when men think they've gotten caught up in something they start telling all sorts of unnecessary lies.

■ The next question was (24) How can we tell if a man is just using us for sex?

Most men said if they end up sleeping with the woman every time, they come by is a good indication, he's using her. And others said if he's always talking about something dealing with sex when he's around you or after you've had sex he gets up and leave.

■ The next question was (25) Why do men leave women just because they've gained weight?

Most men said when women start gaining weight, they get big bellies and becomes unattractive to them. And others said her weight begins to affect their sex life and it causes them to become sexually depressed. But women said they would never leave a man just because he gained weight, because he's still the same person just more for them to love.

■ The next question was (26) Do men love stronger than a woman if so, why?

Most men feel they love just as strong as a woman or more, because they will hurt someone to protect her. And others said they believe women love stronger than men, because a woman can recover from an emotional setback and get back in the relationship like it bever happened. But women feel they love stronger than men because a man can put them through pure hell, and they'll still be there for him.

■ The next question was (27) Why do men lie to their woman and be honest to their side chick?

Most men said they are honest with their side chick about their relationship because they're just creeping and not planning on leaving their home. Nevertheless, they would lie to their woman because even though they're cheating they still love her and know she probably wouldn't be able to handle the truth and they didn't want to hurt or lose her. But men don't realize what happens in the dark will come to the light and by lying to us about being with another woman, they could end up hurting us more than they know in the long run.

■ The next question asked was (28) How does a woman know if she's satisfying her man?

Most men said if they were satisfied with their woman she would know because she would see it in their actions, because besides being happy they would be more intimate and would stay at home a lot more. But women feel if they're sexually active and taking care of home their man should be satisfied.

■ The next question asked was (29) When a man gets in a committed relationship why is it so hard to let go of social media?

Most men feel like FB is a way where they can conversate with different women on social media, and even though they've gotten in a committed relationship it's hard to let go of it because they still desire that attention. omen feel if a man truly love them and is ready to enter a committed relationship, she should be the only woman he desires attention from.

■ The next question asked was (30) If in a relationship and have an opportunity to cheat without getting caught what would you do?

Most men said if they weren't being satisfied at home they probably would cheat. And others said they wouldn't cheat because they're not cheaters. But women feel if you're in a relationship you shouldn't sleep with someone just because it's convenient because a moment of pleasure could cause you a lifetime of pain.

■ The next question asked was (31) How can a man claim to be in love with two women at the same time?

Most men said it's possible to be in love with two women at the same time because they may have the same feelings for them both. But women said regardless of how men may feel there is no way they can be in love with two women at the same time because every woman possess their own unique personality, therefore it's likely he loved one and had lust for the other. And by sleeping with them both its possible he gained feelings but it's likely he's not in love with either of them because if you love someone you want to share your whole being with only that one person.

■ The next question was (32) Why can't men be honest when we ask them questions?

Men don't feel like women can handle the truth, for example, one man said his woman asked him a question and when he tried to be honest, it caused their relationship to suffer drastically and eventually end. Therefore, for men to avoid any mishaps that can result from being honest they choose to tell women whatever it takes to avoid the drama. However, men need to understand that women already know the answers to whatever they've asked, and it only upsets them more when the man lies. Men need to be honest and tell women the truth no matter how much it may hurt, because it's not how you answer the question it's the way you answer it (hint) apologetic.

■ The next question was (33) Why do men date women outside their race?

Most men said that race don't have anything to do with who they're attracted too, but they did say Caucasian and Asian women cater to their needs more than black women, and they don't put them through so much drama either. But speaking as an African American woman men need to understand that all women are the same regardless of their race. All women demand the same respect it's just that white and Asian women handle their situations differently. For example, they tend to avoid confrontations with their men whereas black women welcome it.

■ The next question was (34) Why can't men sympathize with women that have trust issues?

Most men said they can't deal with women with trust issues because no matter how good they try to be she will always bring up what another man has done. They also said they were tired of being blamed for another man's action, because whenever a woman has been hurt every time, a red flag goes up she would treat him as if he was the one who hurt her. It takes a strong man to deal with a woman that has trust issues, but it's not like we bring up past issues intentionally we have just been hurt bad and broken down emotionally. And even though we still desire to be in a relationship we will always have flashbacks until we're healed from all the painful issues we endured from our past.

■ The next question asked was (35) Why do men look at a woman differently when she gains weight?

Most men said they're not attracted to big women and when she gained weight they lost their attraction for them. Some men said the women got too comfortable and let herself go and they no longer could do certain things with her like they use too such as sex etc. But women don't think like that when men gain weight, because even though he's gotten bigger, he's still the man they fell in love with.

■ The last question asked was (36) Why do men think it's so easy to trust them again after they've betrayed us?

Most men said they can only hope that the woman can learn to trust them again. Others said if they betrayed us before nine times out of ten, they would probably do it again, because once a cheater always a cheater. But women feel when they're betrayed by their man the hurt never goes away, it just replays in their minds, and from that point on every time he's not around she will be thinking he's with someone else. Not only am I a published author but I'm also the mother of two sons and a devoted wife of many years who've experienced many issues dealing with matters of the heart.

WHILE WRITING THIS BOOK I realized that most of the questions asked by women involved cheating, but this is a new millennium and it's time that women start thinking outside the box. We know if there's something a man can't get at home, he'll end up getting it from another woman, so as women we need to transform ourselves into the kind of woman that can fit all our man's needs. It's a must that we start doing things that we normally felt was degrading when it comes to sex, because the bottom line is all men want a lady in the streets and a freak in the sheets. And by satisfying all our man's sexual desires he will no longer have a reason to cheat, because he'll be getting everything he needs from home. And contrary to the responses that women gave I must defer because we as women want men to do things we wouldn't do ourselves.

As a woman, I know there was plenty times I've tried to control my relationships only to find myself hurt or even alone. I can recall, being upset with my man for weeks behind something petty and would take the argument to the extreme before I would apologize and admit I was wrong. As women when it comes to relationships, we want men to be damn near perfect when in fact we won't do half the things we want them to do. And women are quick to call men liars and cheaters but if the truth be told a man can't touch a woman when it comes to lying nor cheating, because there have been many times that I've lied and taken things to the extreme to get my way not caring about who I hurt along the way. And when it comes to cheating women are quick to say that men are wrong to cheat on them, but a man can only do what a woman allow, and if tempted long enough the average man would give in too temptation. But women are the best deceivers because even though we know how it feels for a man to cheat on us, we wouldn't hesitate to issue that same pain to someone else if we wanted to cheat bad enough. But unlike men a woman can cheat for years and never get caught because in our minds we find a valid reason for why we're cheating, and even if it's just for self-gratification we would continue cheating regardless of the outcome.

The same love and respect we require from men is the same thing we should be willing to give back in return. I know women may not understand why I'm saying these things, but for a change to occur someone must step forward and speak the truth.

It's always a sensitive subject when it comes to matters of the heart because most women have been hurt and it's easier for them to place the blame on the man instead of seeing it for what it really is. We must understand there are two sides to every story and most of the time women play a major role in the problem but don't want to take ownership for what they've done. But on the same note after surveying different men I've concluded that no matter what women do to please a man; they will never be satisfied with just one woman because the sad truth is men enjoy the hunt.

This is the new millennium and times have changed and if men and women don't come together and put some serious effort into addressing these issues there will only be more pain and heartaches for generations to come.

THE END

JANICE STAMPLEY ALLEN is an inspirational speaker and author of six books titled, "Poetry for the Soul vol 1, 2 and 3, and autobiographies titled, "A Search for Love," "Children Bedtime Stories," and "Resisting Temptation." Within these anointed books Janice shares her personal experiences dealing with abuse and betrayal. These traumatic events led Janice to formulate a book that could answer the many questions that has piqued the curiosity of women even from the beginning of time.

Throughout this book you will see through God's grace and mercy, how Janice was given the ability to use these traumatic experiences to formulate a rare book, that could give women that's going through some trying times a better understanding of God's love. This is a rare book that you will not be able to put down because it reveals the heartfelt responses to the many questions that women all around the world have always wanted to know about men.

www.ingramcontent.com/pod-product-compliance
Lightning Source LLC
Chambersburg PA
CBHW071230140726
47996CB00004B/1547